01 -

M R DEQUAINE
1089 OREGON ST.
GREEN BAY, WIS

W. H. HUDSON: BIRD-MAN

W. H. Hudson: Bird-Man

By

HAROLD GODDARD

E. P. DUTTON & COMPANY
PUBLISHERS :: NEW YORK

FIRST EDITION

W. H. HUDSON: BIRD-MAN

W. H. HUDSON: BIRD-MAN

Lovers of poetry will remember Robert Frost's little poem, *The Road Not Taken:*

Two roads diverged in a yellow wood,
And sorry I could not travel both
And be one traveler, long I stood
And looked down one as far as I could
To where it bent in the undergrowth;

Then took the other, as just as fair,
And having perhaps the better claim,
Because it was grassy and wanted wear;
Though as for that the passing there
Had worn them really about the same,

And both that morning equally lay
In leaves no step had trodden black.
Oh, I kept the first for another day!
Yet knowing how way leads on to way,
I doubted if I should ever come back.

I shall be telling this with a sigh
Somewhere ages and ages hence:
Two roads diverged in a wood, and I—
I took the one less traveled by,
And that has made all the difference.

One of the many ways in which this poem may be taken, I like to think, is as a sort of biological parable. Life on the earth is endlessly diversified; but what any form is to-day is due to the fact that on the hundreds of occasions in the past when it stood where two roads diverged it took this road rather than that, this road again rather than that, and so on and so on. The cumulative effect of all those choices "made all the difference." So far as man is concerned it has always seemed to me that one of the most interesting of these critical moments was when the reptiles—or the radical wing of the reptiles rather—had to decide whether to become birds or mammals. The reptile had four legs. But two were sufficient. Should the other two be used for flight or for grasping tools and weapons? Hands or wings? That was the question. Doubtless those hesitating reptiles, like Robert Frost in his poem, were sorry they could not travel both roads and be one traveller (as, incidentally, they might have, if they had only had six legs instead of four). But that was impossible. So the decision was made, and so far as man was concerned it was settled that he should be a grasping rather than a soaring animal. But there is evidence that man has never quite forgotten that other alternative. The singular fascination that bird life has always had for him, the envy of all inhabitants of the sky that has finally driven him to his own hopelessly inferior mechanical equivalent of flight, the vague belief that is forever reappearing in his folklore and religion in the possibility of the winged man, the fairy or the angel: these things measure the depth of his regret for "the road not taken." I doubt if this longing has ever been given more beautiful expression than in the figure of Rima in W. H. Hudson's *Green Mansions*: Rima, the bird-girl of the forest, that creature who combined all the charm and gentleness of feminine human nature with all the wildness, the brightness, and the loveliness of the birds. But if Rima is the bird-girl, her creator, in whose image she was made, is the bird-man. So true is this that there are moments when in thinking of Hudson he seems less like a man than a specimen of a new human species. His younger brother, after he had said his final farewell to Hudson when the latter was leaving South America for England, added, as Hudson puts it, "this one more last word:

'Of all the people I have ever known you are the only one I don't know.' " His friend and biographer, Morley Roberts, complains at the outset of his study of Hudson that it is impossible to write of him because he was a mystery. "To catch him," he says, "is like catching the song of birds for a book." And in describing his physical appearance he writes: "Assuredly there was never a more remarkable-looking man. In the street he was as noticeable and as much noted as if he had been an inhabitant of another planet. . . . He looked like a half-tamed hawk which at any moment might take to the skies and return no more to those earth-bound creatures with whom he had made his temporary home." There are touches, too, in Hudson of the wild creatures of the earth as well as of the sky. The titles of a number of his books are, consciously or unconsciously, symbolic: *A Hind in Richmond Park*, for instance. Hudson was that hind. But possibly the best expression of this—what shall I call it?—apartness from humanity of the man is to be found in the words of an English critic who speaks of "the temperament of W. H. Hudson, the most beautiful thing God ever made." Lovers of Hudson will pardon the presumption of that utterance.

And yet all this gives a one-sided impression. For Hudson was the most human of men. He was "A Traveller in Little

Things," as well as "A Hind in Richmond Park." So simple was he that he
made friends immediately with the coun-
try folk he constantly met on his tramps,
with children and old people, with the
families in whose homes he stayed in
preference to inns and taverns. Villagers
and people close to the land—he liked
them best and was like one of them himself. The simplicity that this implies is
what makes him as few others an author
for the whole family. Around the fire a
book of his will often hold three genera-
tions, child and grandfather and all
between.

Like the common man, yet at the same
time quite utterly unlike the common

man, this is what Hudson somehow succeeds in being. And it is the likeness that makes the unlikeness so alluring. There is no more fascinating question than the question into what will humanity evolve, and none in the abstract perhaps more futile; while if we attempt to be concrete by picking out our superman from among the geniuses, Plato, Leonardo, or Napoleon, according to taste, somehow these extraordinary persons seem like biological sports or freaks, too few and too far removed from the average of our species to be the starting point or goal for a new humanity. But it is different with a genius like Hudson. Hudsons may be rare; but there is something of what I may call Hudsonian man in most of us. Hudson himself in fact was the product of happy circumstance and wise upbringing as well as of lucky heredity.* Unlikely as such an event may be, there is nothing inherently absurd, then, in imagining man, *homo sapiens*, evolving in the direction of bird-man, homo Hudsonius. If the notion does not seem too fantastic, let us

---

* Hudson was born in 1841 in the Argentine Republic near Buenos Aires. His father, a sheep raiser, was English, his mother American, a New Englander. Hudson had a youth of exceptional freedom, not a little of it spent in the saddle riding carefree over the pampas. Overtaxing his strength when driving cattle in a storm, he had a severe illness that left him with heart trouble from which he suffered the rest of his life. After the death of his parents, Hudson, at the age of twenty-nine, left the Argentine for England. There he studied nature, birds especially, and wrote, his wife helping to support them by taking boarders and giving music lessons. Not until well past middle life did Hudson achieve anything like recognition. Indeed his genius is not yet appreciated. He died in 1922 at the age of eighty-one.

approach Hudson from this angle, keeping in the background of our minds, at any rate, as we discuss him, these two questions: How would our human world be altered, if a generous sprinkling of Hudsonian men were suddenly to appear in it? And conversely, what alterations in our present conceptions and practices would be conducive to the survival and success of such Hudsonian men, if they appeared?

It is certain, to begin with, that in a Hudsonian world the relation between childhood and manhood would be reversed. The effort of education would no longer be to train the boy to be a man but rather to find the secret of letting the man remain a boy. "My life ended at twenty-nine," Hudson was accustomed to say, meaning by that, not that he ceased enjoying life at twenty-nine—he enjoyed it intensely to eighty-one—but that the whole bent and color of his after life was determined by his childhood in the Argentine and by those days of his later youth spent, sometimes from sunrise to sundown, in the saddle, riding in utter freedom over the pampas. John Masefield, in his poem *Biography*, complains that biographers reduce a man's life to lists of dates and facts, missing the mark by emphasizing

> "The power of boredom in the dead
> man's deeds,
> Not the bright moments of the
> sprinkled seeds."

The bright moments of the sprinkled seeds: that is a perfect description of Hudson's marvellous story of his early life with its inspired title, *Far Away and Long Ago*. Of these seminal moments perhaps the most critical in his life was the one when his mother, anxious because her child had fallen into the habit of wandering off by himself and being gone for hours, followed him one day and found him standing rapt and motionless, watching and listening to the birds. Another mother, however sympathetic, might have made her pres-

ence known and marred what was, literal-
ly, the germination of the boy's soul.
Hudson's mother was wise enough to
withdraw unnoticed. The act was char-
acteristic and is the clue, I take it, so far as
parental attitude is concerned, to the pro-
duction of Hudsonian men. Hudson
says as much himself in a passage in his
autobiography that brings out his belief
that the child belongs, as it were, to a
different species from the adult.

"When I think of her," he writes of
his mother, "I remember with gratitude
that our parents seldom or never punished
us, and never, unless we went too far in
our domestic dissensions or tricks, even
chided us. This, I am convinced, is the

right attitude for parents to observe, modestly to admit that nature is wiser than they are, and to let their little ones follow, as far as possible, the bent of their own minds, or whatever it is they have in place of minds.   It is the attitude of the sensible hen toward her ducklings, when she has had frequent experience of their incongruous ways, and is satisfied that they know best what is good for them; though, of course, their ways seem peculiar to her, and she can never entirely sympathize with their fancy for going into the water. I need not be told that the hen is after all only step-mother to the ducklings, since I am contending that the civilized woman —the artificial product of our self-imposed

conditions—cannot have the same relation to her offspring as the uncivilized woman really has to hers. The comparison,
therefore, holds good, the mother with us
being practically step-mother to children
of another race; and if she is sensible, and
amenable to nature's teaching, she will
attribute their seemingly unsuitable ways
and appetites to the right cause, and not to
a hypothetical perversity or inherent de-
pravity of heart, about which many
authors will have spoken to her in many
books:

> But though they wrote it all by rote
> They did not write it right."

This attitude of hands off on the part of his parents so far as the child's deepest interests were concerned, the boy's own extraordinarily sensitive temperament, and one of the most favored spots in the world for watching bird life resulted in a child of civilization attaining a training of the senses comparable to that of the savage, as though, to revert to the imagery of Robert Frost's poem, he had been able to travel both roads and be one traveller. "I rejoiced in colours," Hudson writes of this time, "in colours, scents, sounds, in taste and touch: the blue of the sky, the verdure of earth, the sparkle of sunlight on water, the taste of milk, of fruit, of honey, the smell of dry or moist soil, of wind and rain, of herbs and flowers; the mere feel of a blade of grass made me happy; and there were certain sounds and perfumes, and above all certain colours in flowers, and in the plumage and eggs of birds, such as the purple polished shell of the tinamou's egg, which intoxicated me with delight.   When, riding on the plain, I discovered a patch of scarlet verbenas in full bloom, the creeping plants covering an area of several yards, with the moist, green sward sprinkled abundantly with the shining flower-bosses, I would throw myself from my pony with a cry of joy to lie on the turf among them and feast my sight on their brilliant colour."   To this sheer animal delight in nature was added, a little later, a mystical animistic rapture so intense, he tells us, that the sight of a magnificent sunset would sometimes be almost more than he could endure and would make him wish to hide himself away. Everyone, I suppose, remembers from his childhood moments of similar ecstasy. But in most of us these emotions and instincts are quickly inhibited. In Hudson they remained awake and alert. Out of them developed that extraordinary faculty for accurate and loving observation that, when we read him, makes us feel that we have no eyes, no ears, and, most of all, no noses. "Hudson once told a friend of mine," writes Edward Garnett, "that if he watched a London sparrow he could distinguish it from all other sparrows when it came again." He could often, too, discriminate the voices of individual birds of the same species, just as you and I recognize and distinguish the voices of our friends. His account in *Birds and Man* of his power, after the passage of a quarter of a century, to recall the cries and songs of the hundreds of species of birds that he had known in South America would tax our credulity if we did not trust his absolute veracity on such points. And his sense of smell was just as keen. There are fragrances, he tells us, that fill him with love like that a woman can inspire. "I love to spend entire days," he writes, and he is speaking here not of his early but of his later life, "roaming about on boggy or marshy heaths, perhaps less for what I see and hear of wild life than for the sake of the odour of golden withy or sweet gale, where there are acres of it, and I can stand knee-deep among its thick-growing shrubs and rub my hands and face with the crushed leaves and fill my pockets with them so as to wrap myself up in the delicious aroma." Hundreds of similar passages in Hudson's works show how fully certain instincts flowered in him which in you and me and most other "civilized" men were frozen almost before they were fairly budded. And out of these instincts developed his capacity to enter into the very souls of what we in our condescending fashion are pleased to call the lower animals. "If cows could talk," a little girl of seven or eight once remarked to me as she and I stood watching two of those placid creatures chewing their cuds under a tree, "if cows could talk, nobody knows what new stuff would come into the world." Her observation was a very philosophical one, and it would indeed be both delightful and enlightening if cows could learn to speak our human language, preferably English. But that seems Utopian. So in the meantime, it appears necessary, if we would set up communication with the animals, for us to learn their language. And that is precisely what W. H. Hudson did, especially in the case of birds. With the result, to use my little friend's phrase, that a great deal of new stuff came into the world.

The biologists of the nineteenth century taught us, as a matter of intellectual conviction, man's place in nature. They effected a Copernican revolution. With utter disregard of his dignity, they toppled *homo sapiens* from his throne at the center of creation, showing that he is one bough only on the tree of life, one among hundreds of thousands of living forms each just as significant doubtless from its own point of view as man is in his own estimation. It is easy to assent to all this intellectually. It is the distinction of Hudson that he makes us realize it emotionally and practically—begin to realize it at any rate. Read his essay "My Friend the Pig" and before you are done you will be deluded into thinking that you have actually been talking with a pig and ready to agree with the author that the pig is the most intelligent and democratic of the beasts, "not excepting the elephant and the anthropoid ape," the dog being unworthy of so much as mention in the same connection. Read "The Toad as Traveller" and receive practical instructions in the art of striking up an acquaintance with a lowly amphibian. Read "The Puma," read it to your small son or daughter, as I did to mine—or rather do not read it unless you are willing to be pestered for days, as I was, with demands for a pet puma, so like an immense kitten had the author's sympathetic treatment made this remarkable animal seem to the child.   And so on, up and down the zoölogical scale, from mammal to insect, until we gain such confidence in Hudson's power to penetrate the animal soul that we are willing to take his unsupported word for the fact that he has a perfectly authentic case of telepathy between animal and animal.   Hudson was especially fond of turning his knowledge of the animal mind to the defense of those of our fellow creatures who have generally excited in man the emotions of fear, loathing, or contempt.   I have cited the chapter on "My Friend the Pig." Other examples are "A Noble Wasp," "Facts and Thoughts About Spiders," "A Friendly Rat," "The Bruised Serpent," "The Ass in Fable and Folk-Story," and "Geese, An Appreciation." Only by quoting one of these entire could an idea be conveyed of the extraordinary union of patient observation and loving insight that characterizes Hudson's work. Here is a man who is bent on looking at the world with his own eyes, freshly, directly, face to face, unawed by scientific authority, uninfluenced by popular tradition. Take, for example, his discussion of the goose. Tradition makes the goose a ridiculous figure, a synonym for stupidity. Hudson so far re-

verses this as to make the bird almost sub-
lime. I said a brief quotation would be
inadequate. But we can get at least an
inkling of the effect from his account of
a pair of geese seen in a wild and lonely
district on the southern frontier of Buenos
Aires. It was some days after the immense flocks of these birds who inhabit
this region during the cold months had de-
parted. But here was this single pair,
male and female, a white bird and a
brown one. "The female," Hudson goes
on, "was walking steadily on in a souther-
ly direction, while the male, greatly excited, and calling loudly from time to
time, walked at a distance ahead, and constantly turned back to see and call to his

mate, and at intervals of a few minutes he would rise up and fly, screaming, to a distance of some hundreds of yards; then finding that he had not been followed, he would return and alight at a distance of forty or fifty yards in advance of the other bird, and begin walking on as before. The female had one wing broken, and, unable to fly, had set out on her long journey to the Megallanic Islands on her feet; and her mate, though called to by that mysterious imperative voice in his breast, yet would not forsake her; but flying a little distance to show her the way, and returning again and again, and calling to her with his wildest and most piercing cries, urged her still to spread her wings and fly with him to their distant home.   And in that sad, anxious way they would journey on to the inevitable end, when a pair or family of carrion eagles would spy them from a great distance— the two travellers left far behind by their fellows, one flying, the other walking; and the first would be left to continue the journey alone."   The cumulative effect of scores of such anecdotes in Hudson's works is overwhelming.   They involve an element too intangible for science in its ordinary signification to take into account. But he who would understand life will reckon ill if he leaves it out.

There is a passage in *Birds and Man* that makes singularly clear the distinction between the kind of knowledge that science can attain and the kind of knowledge at which Hudson aimed. He introduces it by a sort of parable in which he tells of a traveller who "in his wanderings in a thinly settled district . . . arrived at a village where, passing by the church, his attention was attracted by a curious spectacle. The church was a big building with a rounded roof, and great blank windowless walls, and the only door he could see was no larger than the door of a cottage. From this door as he looked a small old man came out with a large empty sack in his hands. He was very old, bowed and bent with infirmities, and his long hair and beard were white as snow.　Toddling out to the middle of the churchyard he stood still, and grasping the empty sack by its top, held it open between his outstretched arms for a space of about five minutes; then with a sudden movement of his hands he closed the sack's mouth, and still grasping it tightly, hurried back to the church as fast as his stiff joints would let him, and disappeared within the door.　By and by he came forth again and repeated the performance, and then again, until the traveller approached and asked him what he was doing.　'I am lighting the church,' said the old man; and he then went on to explain that it was a large and a fine church, full of rich ornaments, but very dark inside—so dark that when people came to service the greatest confusion prevailed, and they could not see each other or the priest, nor the priest them. It had always been so, he continued, and it was a great mystery; and he had been engaged by the fathers of the village a long time back, when he was a young man, to carry sunlight in to light the interior; but though he had grown old at his task, and had carried in many, many thousands of sackfuls of sunlight every year, it still remained dark, and no one could say why it was so."

"Parables of this kind as a rule," says Hudson commenting on the story, "can have no moral or hidden meaning in an age so enlightened as this; yet oddly enough we do find among us a delusion resembling that of the villagers who thought they could convey sunshine in a sack to light their dark church." And he gives this example:

"A man walking by the water-side sees by chance a kingfisher fly past, its colour a wonderful blue, far surpassing in beauty and brilliancy any blue he has ever seen in sky or water, or in flower or stone, or any other thing. No sooner has he seen than he wishes to become the possessor of that rare loveliness, that shining object which, he fondly imagines, will be a continual delight to him and to all in his house,—an ornament comparable to that splendid stone which the poor fisherman found in a fish's belly, which was his children's plaything by day and his candle by night. Forthwith he gets his gun and shoots it, and has it stuffed and put in a glass case. But it is no longer the same thing: the image of the living sunlit bird flashing past him is in his mind and creates a kind of illusion when he looks at his feathered mummy, but the lustre is not visible to others.

"It is because of the commonness of this delusion that stuffed kingfishers, and other brilliant species, are to be seen in the parlours of tens of thousands of cottages all over the land. Nor is it only those who live in cottages that make this mistake; those who care to look for it will find that

it exists in some degree in most minds—
the curious delusion that the lustre which
we see and admire is in the case, the coil,
the substance which may be grasped, and
not in the spirit of life which is within, the
atmosphere and miracle-working sunlight
which are without."

It is indeed true, as Hudson says, that it
is not just those who dwell in cottages who
make this mistake. Science herself, intoxicated by her success, is continually
making it, and in so far as our age bows
down to science blindly it may be said to
be the arch-delusion of our time. Hudson helps dispel it, for as the living dart-
ing kingfisher lit by the sunlight is to the
stuffed bird, so is nature in a book of Hud-

son's to nature dissected and classified in the ordinary scientific treatise. Not that Hudson was not scientific in his own procedure. No scientist could possibly have surpassed him as a thorough and conscientious collector and sifter of facts. Of naturalists who are fertile in hypotheses but "shy" on evidence he says: "To be able thus to skim with the swallow's grace over dark and possibly unfathomable questions is a very engaging accomplishment, and apparently a very popular one." His plans for "The Book of the Serpent," a volume that he projected but did not live to write, give us a glimpse of his method. He tells of the thousands of books to be read or consulted, and ten thousand periodicals and annals and proceedings and journals of many natural history societies, great and small, of many countries. And after all this research, with the classification and indexing of notes, would come the task of selection and compression—for "The Book of the Serpent" was to be in one volume rather than six—and the process of digestion and assimilation, until, to use Hudson's words, "the personal impressions of a hundred independent observers, field-naturalists and travellers, and of a hundred independent students of ophiology, would be fused, as it were, and run into one along with the author's personal observations and his deductions." Yet all this would fall short, he declares,

unless those personal observations includ-
ed a first-hand acquaintance with "all the
most distinguished ophidians of the
globe." "The first sight of a thing," he
says, "the shock of emotion, the vivid and
ineffaceable image registered in the brain,
is worth more than all the knowledge ac-
quired by reading, and this applies to the
serpent above all creatures. There is indeed but little difference between this creature dead and in confinement."

"The Book of the Serpent" was never
written. But "The Book of the Birds"
was, in many volumes, and in each of
them Hudson followed this method of ex-
tracting the quintessence of innumerable
facts. "Birds at Their Best" is the signifi-

cant title of the first chapter of *Birds and Man*. In it he tells us that he sees birds mentally in two ways: each species he has known in its wild state has its type in his mind—an image which he invariably sees when he thinks of the species; and, in addition, one, or two, or several, or more, images of the same species as it appeared to him at some exceptionally favorable moment and was viewed with peculiar interest and pleasure. The first, generalized image of the species might well, it seems to me, stand for the scientific method; the other individualized images of particular birds at their best representing that Hudsonian something that is not so much opposed to science as added to it.

There is a passage in his chapter, "White of Selborne," in which Hudson, for once, puts explicitly the idea that is implicit in the attitude and passages which we have been discussing. He is speaking of the change of outlook that the general acceptance of the doctrine of evolution has brought, pointing out how evolution, having wrought in our minds, is at last entering our souls, setting up a new relationship between facts and knowledge. "We are bound as much as ever to facts," he says, "we seek for them more and more diligently, knowing that to break from them is to be carried away by vain imaginations. All the same, facts in themselves are nothing to us; they are important only

in their relations to other facts and things
—to all things and the essence of things,
material and spiritual. We are not like
children gathering painted shells and
pebbles on a beach; but, whether we
know it or not, are seeking after something beyond and above knowledge. The
wilderness in which we are sojourners is
not our home; it is enough that its herbs
and roots and wild fruits nourish and give
us strength to go onward. Intellectual
curiosity, with the gratification of the individual for its only purpose, has no place
in this scheme of things as we conceive it.
Heart and soul are with the brain in all in-
vestigation—a truth which some know in
rare, beautiful intervals, and others

never." This truth is indeed rarely present to most of us, but if we were to judge by his works we could well believe that it was never absent from Hudson's mind. It colors and pervades his writings from end to end until we grow convinced that in a world of Hudsonian men art and science would no longer, as so often with us, be at cross purposes, but would disappear, as it were, by being taken up into a higher category for which we have at present no adequate name.

If this conception, as Hudson suggests, is one natural to our age, we should expect to run on it in other writers of kindred philosophy or spirit. We do. And it is interesting to compare one or two other formulations of it with Hudson's. Thoreau tells us in one of his journals that he has two commonplace books, one for facts and one for poetry. "But I find it difficult," he goes on, "always to preserve the vague distinction which I had in my mind, for the most interesting and beautiful facts are so much the more poetry, and that is their success. They are translated from earth to heaven. I see that if my facts were sufficiently vital and significant, perhaps transmuted more into the substance of the human mind, I should need but one book of poetry to contain them all." Facts at Their Best, he might have called it.

Another man who has said the same

thing in very different language is Samuel Butler. (Hudson, by the way, with that eye that genius has for genius, recognized the greatness of Butler long before he was known to literary England.) Butler, in *Life and Habit*, discussing the relationship between consciousness and knowledge, lays down the paradoxical proposition that there is always something elementary, awkward, or even ugly in knowledge that has not become, as it were, reflex. A man cannot walk gracefully until he ceases to be aware that he is walking. The same, says Butler, is true of thinking.

"If the reader hesitates," he continues, "let him go down into the streets and look in the shop-windows at the photographs of eminent men, whether literary, artistic, or scientific, and note the work which the consciousness of knowledge has wrought on nine out of every ten of them; then let him go to the masterpieces of Greek and Italian art, the truest preachers of the truest gospel of grace; let him look at the Venus of Milo, the Discobolus, the St. George of Donatello. If it had pleased these people to wish to study, there was no lack of brains to do it with; but imagine 'what a deal of scorn' would 'look beautiful' upon the Venus of Milo's face if it were suggested to her that she should learn to read. Which, think you, knows most, the Theseus, or any modern professor taken at random? True, the advancement of learning must have had a great share in the advancement of beauty, inasmuch as beauty is but knowledge perfected and incarnate—but with the pioneers it is *sic vos non vobis*; the grace is not for them, but for those who come after. Science is like offences. It must needs come, but woe unto that man through whom it comes; for there cannot be much beauty where there is consciousness of knowledge, and while knowledge is still new it must in the nature of things involve much consciousness.

"It is not knowledge, then, that is incompatible with beauty; there cannot be too much knowledge, but it must have passed through many people who it is to

be feared must be more or less disagreeable,
before beauty or grace will have anything
to say to it; it must be so incarnate in a
man's whole being that he shall not be
aware of it, or it will fit him constrainedly
as one under the law, and not as one under
grace."

"Incarnate in a man's whole being":
that is a perfect description of Hudson's
knowledge, upon the pages of whose
works truth and beauty become indistin-
guishable, and while he does not attain to
that divine summit to which Butler points
in his suggestion that gods and goddesses
would never condescend to learn to read or
write, still, he is forever expressing a
healthy skepticism of the printed page, so

that as compared with Butler's university professor he is indisputably a creature of a higher species.

This doctrine of the immanence of knowledge within beauty helps explain the extraordinary concourse of thoughts upon a thousand subjects that are to be found just beneath the surface of a group of works ostensibly on natural history. Not until the publication of *A Hind in Richmond Park*, his last book, did some people realize, I imagine, the range and scope of Hudson's interests: physiology, psychology, anthropology, philosophy, poetry, art, these and a dozen other subjects jostle one another indiscriminately as Hudson discusses telepathy and the wind and the history of English literature and the sense of smell and the evolution of instrumental music and innumerable other themes and questions. All this, however, was no revelation to the attentive reader of Hudson's previous works. It was in them, too, albeit a little less explicit. It was there between the lines, there as overtones and undertones, there in solution, there in the form of Thoreau's facts transmuted into poetry or Butler's unconscious, might we not better say, superconscious knowledge. That is why Hudson is so much more than an ornithologist and naturalist, why, whatever your own interest, provided only it is vital and human, you can find light reflected on it from

Hudson's pages.   For instance: he gives a purely objective account of how two sparrow hawks that he watched for weeks brought up their young, and lo! whatever he himself intended, the passage fairly bristles with suggestions for the human parent or educator.   He writes a chapter, "Mary's Little Lamb," about a lamb brought up among dogs, and while it is in a form that would hold the attention of a small child it probes deeper into the problem of heredity and environment than many a learned treatise on that subject. His chapters in *A Traveller in Little Things* on "Little Girls I Have Met" are among the most delicately beautiful things about childhood in the language, so delightful that we do not notice what a contribution they are to child psychology, not to mention how they confirm Butler's view of the superiority of unconscious over conscious knowledge. The majority of his essays on bird and animal life are alive with suggestions to those interested in the social and political problems of man. Of Hudson one may say as Meredith did of Melampus:

"For him the woods were a home and gave
    him the key
  Of knowledge, thirst for their treasures in
    herbs and flowers.
The secrets held by the creatures nearer than
    we
  To earth he sought, and the link of their
    lives with ours."

Sociologists, both amateur and professional, are too prone to forget that life has conducted other experiments on this planet than the human one and that it is the height of foolishness for man, in endeavoring to shape his own future, to leave out of account nature's thousands of other attempts, of all degrees of success and failure, to solve problems quite like those that confront humanity. This truth, we feel, was perpetually in the back of Hudson's brain, for it pervades his works like an atmosphere. Only rarely, as in his essay on "The Strange Instincts of Cattle," does he allow it to come into the foreground. "Some gregarious animals, particularly birds," he says in this essay, "live together in the most perfect peace and amity; and there is no leader required, because in their long association together as a species in flocks, they have attained to a oneness of mind, so to speak, which causes them to move or rest, and to act at all times harmoniously together, as if controlled and guided by an extraneous force. I may mention that the kindly instinct in animals, which is almost universal between male and female in the vertebrates, is most apparent in these harmoniously acting birds. . . . Naturally among such kinds no one member is of more consideration than another. But among mammals such equality and harmony is rare. The instinct of one and all is to lord it over the others, with the result that one more powerful or domineering gets the mastery, to keep it thereafter as long as he can." Plainly the birds, or some of them, have solved the peace problem, have reconciled liberty with society, have achieved a leaderless democracy that is not a mob. Is it impudent to suggest that some of our human "authorities" on these questions might turn their attention with profit to ornithology, ornithology, I mean, of the Hudsonian brand?

This wisdom of earth on which he relied Hudson loves to summon in rebuke of the intellectual pride of man. His attachment to all wild and primitive life was scarcely deeper than was his contempt for

men in crowds and cities, with their round
of petty business and pleasure, their jeal-
ousies, their book learning, their vaunted
progress. Civilization was poison to him,
nothing less. Its contaminating touch
kept him from loving quite unreservedly
even such innocent things as cultivated
flowers. He likes nothing better than to
bring nature into fierce contrast with
civilized man, often not without a note
of bitterness bordering on cynicism that
sounds strange enough in the voice of
this lover of birds and little girls. "The
blue sky," he writes in *Hampshire Days*,
"the brown soil beneath, the grass, the
trees, the animals, the wind, the rain, and
sun, and stars are never strange to me; for

I am in and of and am one of them; and my flesh and the soil are one, and the heat in my blood and in the sunshine are one, and the winds and tempests and my passions are one. I feel the 'strangeness' only with regard to my fellow-men, especially in towns, where they exist in conditions unnatural to me, but congenial to them; where they are seen in numbers and in crowds, in streets and houses, and in all places where they gather together; when I look at them, their pale civilized faces, their clothes, and hear them eagerly talking about things that do not concern me. They are out of my world—the real world. All that they value, and seek and strain after all their lives long, are the merest baubles and childish things; and their ideals are all false, and nothing but by-products, or growths, of the artificial life—little funguses cultivated in heated cellars." Swift, in his most devastating mood, is scarcely less ingratiating, or the Shakespeare of *Timon* more annihilating, than that. Hudson says the same thing more quietly and pathetically in *A Traveller in Little Things* when he speaks of "those who live not in villages but in dreadful cities" and compares them with "motherless men who have never known a mother's love and have never had a home on earth." It was because he was not motherless that he reads so profoundly the secrets of earth.

But if we are to penetrate to anything like the heart of this man's superconscious wisdom, we must pass from his matter to his manner. We must say something of his style. That style has been the despair of critics. In its presence, dozens of them have thrown up their hands helplessly, exclaiming: "The utter simplicity of it! The transparency! The artlessness! And yet what effects! Where is the secret of it?" And they have no answer.

But Hudson himself has an answer, though of course, in good Butlerian fashion, he is not thinking of himself when he offers it. He is asking rather how it happens that simple people with no special scientific or literary equipment not infrequently have a power of penetrating into nature's secrets and of giving expression to them in a manner denied to the professional naturalist who dedicates his life to the study of these very matters. Notice, as you listen to Hudson's words, that from another angle and with far less air of paradox, he is saying precisely the same thing as Samuel Butler. Notice, also, that the passage, without particularly intending to, becomes a text-book on composition condensed into two paragraphs.

Hudson once received a letter, he explains, from a woman who wanted to know whether he could identify from her description an insect in which she was particularly interested. She had seen it

when a child in the garden at her early
home in Wiltshire, and never since, nor
had she ever discovered what it was.
"When I was a child," the letter said, "I
had a great fancy for a rare, strange, fascinating insect called by the children of
my day the Merrylee-dance-a-pole. Only
on the hottest and longest of summer days
did the radiant being delight our eyes; to
have seen it conferred high honour and
distinction on the fortunate beholder. We
regarded it with mingled awe and joy, and
followed its erratic and rapid flight with
ecstasy. It was soft and warm and brown,
fluffy and golden, too, and created in our
infantile minds an indescribable impression of glory, brilliance, aloofness, elusive-

ness. We thought it a being from some other world, and during each of its frequent sudden disappearances among the flowering bushes we held our breath, fearing it would return no more, but had flown right through the blossoming screen and back to the sun and stars. To me it was an apparition of inexpressible delight, and I longed to be a Merrylee-dance-a-pole myself to fly to unheard-of, unthought-of, undreamed-of beautiful flowery lands."

"A descriptive passage this," Hudson comments, "by one who is not a literary person, a student of expression anxiously seeking after the 'explicit word,' yet an expression rare and beautiful as the thing described: one reads it with a quickened pulse. Who should dream of finding its like anywhere in the thousand books of British Butterflies and Moths which our exceedingly industrious lepidopterists have produced during the last six or seven decades? Yet the same thousand volumes were written less for the scientific student of entomology than for the general reader, or for every person who on seeing a white admiral or a privet moth wants to know what it is and goes to a book to find out all about it. These writers all fail in the very thing which one would imagine to be the most important in books intended for such a purpose—the power to convey to the reader's mind a vivid image of the thing described. One would like to know what the professional entomologist or writer of books about moths would say of the passage I have quoted from a letter asking information about an insect. Probably he would say that the lady wrote more from the heart than the head, that writing so she is rhapsodical and as inaccurate as one would expect her to be, although one is able to identify her Merrylee-dance-a-pole as the *Macroglossa stellatarum*.

"It would be perfectly true," Hudson continues, "she is inaccurate, yet succeeds in producing the effect aimed at while the accurate writers fail. She succeeds because she saw the object as a child, emotionally, and after thirty years was still able to recover the precise feeling experienced then and to convey to another the image in her mind. We may say that impressions are vivid and live vividly in the mind, even to the end of life, in those alone in whom something that is of the child survives in the adult—the measureless delight in all this visible world, experienced every day by the millions of children happily born outside the city's gates, but so rarely expressed in literature, as Traherne, let us say, expressed it; and, with the delight, the sense of wonder in all life, which is akin to, if not one with, the mythical faculty, and if experienced in a high degree is a sense of the supernatural in all natural things. We may say, in fact, that unless the soul goes out to meet what we see we do not see it; nothing do we see, not a beetle, not a blade of grass."

It would be hard, even in Hudson, to go beyond that. And yet, close as we are here to the heart of the man, I believe we can get still closer, if we take one further illustration, a case where the speaker— not the writer this time—was a child of ten or eleven and what she said became in a manner the immediate inspiration of one of Hudson's own books: *Birds in Town and Village*.

Walking in May in a London park, he noticed ahead of him three children, two quite small, the third, in whose charge the others were, a robust-looking girl, aged about ten or eleven years. From their

dress and appearance he took them to be
the children of a respectable artisan or
small tradesman; but what chiefly attracted his attention was the very great
pleasure the elder girl appeared to take in
the birds. "She had come well provided
with stale bread to feed them," Hudson
goes on, "and after giving moderately of
her store to the wood-pigeons and sparrows, she went on to the others, native and
exotic, that were disporting themselves in
the water, or sunning themselves on the
green bank. She did not cast her bread
on the water in the manner usual with
visitors, but was anxious to feed all the
different species, or as many as she could
attract to her, and appeared satisfied

when any one individual of a particular kind got a fragment of her bread. Meanwhile she talked eagerly to the little ones, calling their attention to the different birds. Drawing near, I also became an interested listener; and then, in answer to my questions, she began telling me what all these strange fowls were. 'This,' she said, glad to give information, 'is the Canadian goose, and there is the Egyptian goose; and here is the king-duck coming towards us; and do you see that large, beautiful bird standing by itself, that will not come to be fed? That is the golden duck. But that is not its real name; I don't know them all, and so I name some for myself. I call that one the golden duck because in the sun its feathers sometimes shine like gold.' It was a rare pleasure to listen to her, and seeing what sort of a girl she was, and how much in love with her subject, I in my turn told her a great deal about the birds before us, also of other birds she had never seen nor heard of, in other and distant lands that have a nobler bird life than ours; and after she had listened eagerly for some minutes, and had then been silent for a little while, she all at once pressed her two hands together, and exclaimed rapturously, 'Oh, I do so love the birds!'

"I replied that that was not strange, since it is impossible for us not to love whatever is lovely, and of all living things birds were made most beautiful.

"Then I walked away, but could not forget the words she had exclaimed, her whole appearance, the face flushed with colour, the eloquent brown eyes sparkling, the pressed palms, the sudden spontaneous passion of delight and desire in her tone. The picture was in my mind all that day, and lived through the next, and so wrought on me that I could not longer keep away from the birds, which I, too, loved; for now all at once it seemed to me that life was not life without them; that I was grown sick, and all my senses dim; that only the wished sight of wild birds could medicine my vision; that only by drenching it in their wild melody could my tired brain recover its lost vigour."

If anyone thinks this incident of the

child in the London park is trivial and unworthy of the space I have given it, I cannot agree with him. If this is trivial, then
Hudson himself is trivial and most of what
he wrote.   And indeed there will be some
to take that view.   As for me, I have put
this passage last among my quotations because, the more I consider it, the more it
seems to me to incarnate well-nigh all of
his philosophy.   Here, at the foci, as always with Hudson, are the child and the
birds, here is his doctrine as to the place of
the senses and the emotions in education,
here is his ideal of man's attitude toward
other forms of life, here is his conception
of the right relation between observation
and expression, between facts and imagi=

nation in other words, or, more pretentiously, between science and art. But there is something more here also, and that something more is perhaps the most remarkable thing in all Hudson, a thought that, like a star that now shines out and is now obscured, plays through what turned out to be his final utterance about life, the rare and wonderful last chapter of his last book. The chapter was left unrevised and unfinished and its last paragraphs were put together from the author's notes after his death by his friend and biographer, Morley Roberts. This explains in part why it strikes us as fragmentary and tentative, but its lack of finality flows very much more out of the vastness of its theme, which is that of the relation of art to life. Art to Hudson is an inadequate organ for the expression of man's full wonder in life and the beauty of life. He seeks, and he seems to sense the coming of, "something better than art, or at all events more satisfying, not only to the artistic-minded person and to those who specialize in some form of art, but to people generally—to everyone." As Nietzsche sought a realm beyond good and evil, so Hudson seeks a world beyond art and science. I can here only hint at his meaning, and refer you to this very remarkable chapter. I may add, however, that Hudson distrusts the power of the artist, as he does of the scientist, to see things in their right relations, for the artist like the scientist is a specialist. And to specialize, Hudson says, is to lose your soul. They alone can be trusted to see who have no profession, no vocation which absorbs their attention. Of such perfectly untrammeled, emancipated persons he believes there are not a few, though at present they are mainly reticent, inarticulate. But their existence is the evidence of profound evolutionary changes in the human mind—or in certain human minds—the promise of a time when the artist (to still call him that) will no longer use such crude media as clay and pigment and the rest, which after all are like mere toys, but will express life through the medium of life itself, just as the child in the London park did. The woman who wrote the letter about the beautiful moth was an unconscious artist. She did well. But she did even better as a child, as did the other child with whom Hudson talked. *They both reached a point beyond art.* Yet even they, even the children, are only on the way. It is the birds who have arrived, who have achieved the ideal of which Hudson dreams. The birds are strangely absent from that last chapter of *The Hind in Richmond Park*, but the birds, whom Hudson worshipped, are the unconscious source and sanction of its philosophy. Some day, Hudson seems to say, men will live as the birds sing, for life's own sake.